Naked, Alone,

THE LIFE AND TIMES OF CANDACE ELDRIDGE:
Naked, Alone, & Unafraid
BY CANDACE ELDRIDGE

Naked, Alone, & Unafraid

© 2018 by Candace Eldridge

All rights reserved. No part of this publication may be reproduced, stored in a retrieval system, or transmitted in any form or by any means – for example electronic, photocopy, and recording- without the prior written permission of the publisher.

I dedicate this book to me because I was able to step outside of myself and get out of my own way to present my passions to the world.

I dedicate this book to God for allowing me the space, time, creativity to speak my truth via the arts.

I dedicate this book to both my supporters, those who did support or voiced their support, or bought into my passion with their dollars to support. I also dedicate this book to those who spoke support but never supported. Both sides were helpful to me becoming the woman that I am today.

Naked, Alone, & Unafraid

Introduction

At the beginning of 2007, I began to feel the urgency of life. I felt an intense need to accomplish goals, have a relationship that would lead (eventually) to marriage, and to be successful in ministry and in my own business. Up against all of these urges, I felt defeated before I even began in earnest. It seemed as if I would not be able to complete these tasks no matter how hard I tried.

As an avid journal writer, it was normal for me to put my thoughts to pen and paper. My journaling allow me to express thoughts, ideas, prayers, and eventually poems. I began painting after being introduced to the idea of painting for fun and relaxation in a local art studio. My interest and creativity grew, and I began to create my own works of art.

I kept both of these art forms close to my heart as an outward expression of my desire for creativity. Painting and writing taught me how to focus, to shut off all the noises of the world, to let go of worry and doubt. I was one with my art and peaceful within. I did not discover the term *art therapy* until much later, but the completion of almost 200 paintings and too numerous to count poems definitely counts as therapy for me. It was judgeless listener to my insecurities.

It has taken me over ten years to release my total work of art. Not as a result of the lack of completion but out of the desire to not be vulnerable to others thoughts and opinions of my works and me.

I am grateful for maturity to help guide me to a place of peace beyond understanding, and beyond the judgment and opinions of others. I am happy to be in a place where I can stand in the mirror and be proud of the woman staring back at me. This is the best accomplishment I could make in life. As a result, I share my art, my heart, and my inner thoughts straight from my journal. Thank you for sharing this journey with me. As you read my words and view my art, I hope you take the time to do some self-reflection of your own and continue along your journey to be the best "you" that you can possibly be.

This is just the beginning! Thank you! **Candace**

Naked, Alone, & Unafraid

All artwork shown within this book is available in print and/or original canvas painting. Contact Candace Eldridge at CLEARTISTRY@GMAIL.COM regarding any painting you are interested in purchasing by citing the page number. Candace is also available for all custom commission projects as well.

Naked, Alone, & Unafraid

Table of Contents

01/12/06	11
10/22/08	15
Words of Life	17
11/20/09	19
11/17/10	21
11/18/10	24
10/20/10	26
04/21/11	27
05/02/11	30
03/31/12	31
08/20/12	34
I Like	35
08/22/12	37
10/07/12	40
10/22/12	43
12/07/12	45
03/07/13	46
03/18/13	49
04/26/13	51
05/28/13	53
11/20/13	54
The Sky	57
Crash	58
Lily Pad	60
Unending Pain... Or Is It?	62
How? My Questions for God	64
Too Easy	69
IJUSWANASING	74
I'm a Virgin	77
Wanna Be, Wanna Be, Wanna Be Me	79
It's So Simple It's Hard	81
The Introduction	83
My Prayer for Him	86
You Ain't the One	89
A Love Letter to My Daddy	91
We are a Reflection of Your Perfection.	93
Perspective	95
The Hardest Part	96
1:58 PM	99

Purpose Pusher – THANKS!!	100
Mas Y Mas	103
You Make Me Brave	104
Love Who I Love and Hate Who I Hate	106
06/28/15	110
"Me"	112
The Thought	119
Life's Too Short	122
The Treasure of a Woman's Heart	123
Where Do I End & You Begin?	126
Love Takes Time	128
All the Fake Accolades…	130
The Man	131
Inside Out	133
Colors of Blood	137
Conceptualize	139
In or Out	141
Saturated	142
The Blame Game	144
I still believe	146
Speaking Silently	148
Muse	150
Inside The Room	152
I Feel For You	155
Decisions	156
Are You Ready For the Shift?	159
New Meaning of Friendship	161
Naked, Alone, and Unafraid	166

01/12/06

Can you have time to grow?

Is that so impossible for me to let you do?

I cried, and you cringed;

We were both uncomfortable,

Yet we are connected by love

Separated by love

One that is greater than I can give

And you are too small to receive.

If the love of God was not there,

I would have left a long time ago.

I would have taken the way of escape when it was presented.

If the love of God was not there,

You wouldn't have been attracted to me.

You wouldn't have sought to get to know the deeper side of the deep.

If the love of God was not there,

Hope for a future of a present would not have presented itself.

That love that is greater than the great,

Hated by the great,

Though no one is greater than

A love too unfathomable in our sin

Would forgive my inequities and yours if asked

IF that love wasn't there,

There would be no me,

No you,

No us.

No we.

No possibility of having a unity blessed by man for all men to see.

Yet and still I don't know how it be.

I couldn't talk to you

And you wouldn't talk to me.

Could the hurt run so deep that there is no possibility of understanding?

I place no more blame on you than I do me,

But you got to understand that that was four years for me.

Four years of devotion, promise, trust, and lack of love.

Four years for me to find

Find a peace of mind,

Find a place of heart,

Find a how do I do and where I am supposed to be.

Four years of development and release

That is gone.

Not completely but enough to be felt,

And you wonder why I cried.

You wondered why I was quiet,

Why I couldn't talk.

The gravity of my actions placed me in a place of solemn emptiness

that your hugs could not heal.

You shouldn't have done it;

I shouldn't have let you.

But it is done.

After the fact

No jokes could be told.

That was like a piece of my soul that was taken from

Something that was promised and yet that promise I couldn't keep.

Feelings of guilt, hurt, anger, and despair;

Fear of tomorrow

No bearing of who I am or was.

My accomplishment and my lack thereof

Showed my human side of how far I'd come and all that I have endured.

But in that moment between us

All I could think about was God

Setting the stage of who we were going to be

We be separated for who knows when -

A moment, a time, a reality -

But it has to happen, and it has already begun -

One moment came and went like the setting of the sun.

Will it happen again?

No not until the time is right.

A wedding ring, our favorite song, a dance at candlelight:

You sweep me off my feet.

A true prince charming taking me away to your kingdom to be

There we shall be one as we are supposed to be

Under moonlight we will dance, kiss, and be married.

10/22/08

I never imagined you would not be there

I never thought that would be a reality

To tell the truth

It never really crossed my mind

My lack of preparation has thrown me into frenzy

Of emotions covering the gamut and spectrum of colors

Overwhelming, debilitating, confusing all at the same time

I never thought you wouldn't be here or there

Now I fly back to reality check in life

Work, play, church, date, 9 to 5, 6 to 9, 10 to 6 again

Going through each day wondering where

And what I would be if things were done differently

I appreciate the fact that I don't have the answer

That I can go forward in my life knowing your missing

That I feel as deeply as I do

That I'm confused at the same time

I never thought you wouldn't be here

Each day is a new day

I get to wake up and do it again

To try again

It is missing your laugher and smiles

Your bear hugs that suffocated me

You

Its missing you

Cause I never prepared myself with the thought

That I might never see you again

I never thought you wouldn't be here

Naked, Alone, & Unafraid

Words of Life

Words of life creating life of words to be spoken

A painted brush tipped in rhythms and butterflies flowing freely

A breath...

Of air felt in the coldest places

Giving and giving until there is nothing left to give

Measures of love against the qualities of life

Extensions and extending yourself until there is no more

Silently recognizing dreams again

Quietly recognizing them as reality

I give myself away so that you can use me

Being held by your love is a reminder of your arms holding me

If this is crazy and all I have left is faith

Then lock me up in your insanity

This non-married state giving life like a wife

Imagining that you would grant me the ability to be held physically

like when you hold me spiritually

Not giving less of me but more and more and more and more

Allowing my vessels to flow your blood

As you are the master puppeteer and I am but a doll on sticks

Having the comfort to move in your moves relaxes me

Vulnerable enough not to think

Allowing the strings of life, the breath of life

Swinging one... so you can use me

Now that's love... and life and hope.

11/20/09

Too many words take away the imagination

Rivers of flowing waters

Radiant and bright

No need to open my mouth, no words will come out

The flow of my heart precedes me

Not imagination

Not negligence

A peaceful yearning for the more

The greedy desire for the stillness to never leave

Experience of life so new it frightens

Even me, the strong

However, yet and still

It moves me

Distinctly balancing the scales

Adding them on one by one

See the faces as it tips in my favor

An extension of a hand given to assist

Measured and weighed against the tons of grams of truth

Blinded by the letting go of yesterday

And the opportunities to tomorrow's forever more joy and peace

Safe and sanctity

Hope justified in the whisper of a song

Coming and giving

Too hard to imagine

Now I just must experience

Can't speak now

11/17/10

I see you walking aimlessly about

Dead faces

Solemn eyes

Lifelessness

Mundane day to day nothingness

Meaning emptiness un-expressed

How do you live?

Where is your joy?

The beats of your heart come from where?

I understand the feeling

Not happy or sad

Just kind of here

Maintaining all kinds of efforts just to move

Living in a microwave mindset that wants it all now

Not a truth but a false life I live

It's alright

It's ok

It's never enough

Ready to downgrade my existence to the bare minimum

Brush? Check. Paint? Check. Canvas? Check. Pen? Check. Pad? Check. Bubble Yum? No Check!!

I've forgotten my childhood joys

Replacing them with empty voids

Won't ever walk my dog and he is getting fat

Not like Fat Kats or Fat Stacks

But cellulite fat and Kit Kats

I'm getting it back though

The dreams and the joy of my childhood toys

Marker? Check. Scissors? Check. Colored Paper? Check. Ruler? Check. Music? Check.

Ribbons? Check. Tap shoes? Check. Lipstick? Check. Hair tie? Check.

I'm starting to remember my favorite things

Feeling like dancing on the wind

Brilliant colors shadowing the rainbows of life

Clay? Check. Trace? Check. Piano? Check. Tree? Check. Leaves? Check.

Candy coated hidden paths into deep, sweet, secret places? Check, Check, Check!!!

No longer living by the motto of just getting by

Striving for the satisfaction of this world

Give me joy

Give me peace

Give me a piece of cake just for me to eat

But don't give me the endless un-necessities

Of the world which creates these intolerable realities

I don't want to be you

I don't even want to be better than you

As the bottom you know where you stand

I don't need the stuff

Naked, Alone, & Unafraid

Just give me a Mic in my hand

So I can sing

When the dog bites

When the bee's sting

When I'm feeling sad

I simply remember my favorite things

And then I don't feel so bad

11/18/10

I was drawn to you

Not the moment I met you

Minutes later

Conversation ensued

A card game

Dinner

By the end of the night I was ready

To follow you into the twilight

The aroma of your presence was so sweet

Enticing me like a piece of meat

That has been staged for that big girl

Who hasn't ate in 4 days

Or like that puppy who is shown kindness

Everywhere you go he is there

It is so sad that I want to follow you

Yet I don't apologize for it

Your greatness is shouting out for the world to hear

I see heaven responding to the call

That kind of coverage should have everyone chasing after you

I don't think you have yet been presented to the world

You were however presented to me

And I am responding

I see you

Naked, Alone, & Unafraid

I'm drawn to you

As a deer panted for water

How strange for me to feel this way

You have been confirmed in heaven and God never leaves me astray

I wonder where you will lead me....

10/20/10

Hope didn't occur over night
Didn't surface at day's first light
Dreams and the ability to dream
Was cultivated in a thought
And everything will change
Just not when you want
It's never ever the beginning that is the problem
Nor the end of something
All the in between in the middle
Put their stamp on that thang
People so swayed by the troubles of today
That they forget the tomorrows to come
With an attitude of bitterness
A mouth of a sailor
Trouble continues to keep on keeping on

04/21/11

Here I am Lord

Yes I grew tired

I left You and walked away

Making up in my mind

To do things my own way

Never in my heart leaving You

But walking away as only I can

My turning point came when the emptiness engulfed me

I was surrounded by walls and barriers

That I built with my own hands

Tearing them down piece by peace

Not moving because all I see is me surrounded on all sides

Lord

I looked in the mirror and saw my empty reflection

Why did it matter anymore?

All the things that I placed value on

The men, relationships, money, career, lack of self-care, surrounded by emptiness

A slight twinkle in my eye once looked upon more closely

To me to the abyss of my soul

I missed myself Lord

And I can admit

The voice that constantly said there was something wrong with me

I believed

You would think I would know better having all this God Goodness in me

But I fell to the susceptible lies that lived so long within me

Then I began to miss You Lord

Truth is

I always hoped you would receive me back

That the fraud of my character would never be revealed

For others to see

Now I just don't care anymore

I can say that the world left me fleeting with emotionalism

Entitlement

Doubt fear

Anger

Bitterness

No hope

No love for you or me

Or anyone in-between

Feelings of the wind

Nothingness

Of course my fraud came out because it was earth leading and earth bound

First please forgive me for walking away from you

It was not done in love but in spite

And also forgive me for so easily believing others

The not good part of my life

The things that depleted m soul and drowned my faith

Naked, Alone, & Unafraid

Lastly, forgive me for being so mad at you

It's not that I don't see the good out of the circumstances

I am not in

I recognize of course You are and was right

I guess I was just too led by my

Self-ish-ness

That I didn't want to give you credit

You were right and fair in the judgments placed upon me and before

me

I don't say this with spite

But in acknowledging the greater good of everything

That led to today

05/2/11

Everything and everyone says to wait

But I don't have that much patience

Or the time to wait

It seems like it's been forever since

I felt my lover's kiss

Whose love is greater than anyone?

Could ever miss

But he loves me and kisses me

Then he goes outside my reach

As he goes outside of my reach

And I try to chase after him

My frustration arises

Wondering why me

Feeling abandoned and neglected

Forced to find my own way

03/31/12

I finally understand what it feels like

To give your all and feel like a fraud

That what you gave wasn't good enough

For others to understand or care to

All those great people who gave so selfishly

We're not selfish at it

It was just in their DNA to go above and beyond for others

Isn't that what Gandhi did?

Hoping to inspire as well as lead others to realize this path themselves

From within

Isn't that what MLK did?

Giving his life for a cause sacrificing everything in the process

Isn't that what Jesus did?

There is no way around the sacrifice

When you want to do something great on earth

That is what heaven planned for you to do

Will you be more fulfilled?

Enlightened?

Capable

Of Leading

Does it have meaning?

I understand Solomon

I understand his ways

I understand the desire to have a normal day

I know what it felt like

For Jesus to have wept blood

He wanted so badly for those around Him to understand

I now that love hurts

Not regular love

Dating love

Or infatuation

Not that those do not express love authentically

But real love is doing for others when you don't want to but you know it's the right thing to do

To deal with the daily disappointment of not being #1 to someone else or even #5

Being in broad daylight and in the midst of a crowd

Ignored

Until someone wants something from you

That only you can give

No one else

You're the reliable one

While in your own time of need

You get on your knees and cry

Just to let the pain stop hurting

Only to get up and tuck yourself in at night

Ask God, Jesus, and the Holy Spirit to comfort you as you sleep

I understand God

I am getting it

08/20/12

Woke up feeling defeated

Heartbroken

Alone and not knowing when and if that would end

As a result

Tears fell down my face uncontrollably

I didn't want to acknowledge this sadness but here it is again

A lovely birthday cake

Symbolizing the lack of partakers

Stands more than half full

The opportunist sees this as a moment of fellowship

Finding new friends to love

But my heart looks at the emptiness

How the cake could be my demise if ate alone

As "That's what friends are for is played in the background of my mind"

I extend another invitation to invite others in

Another and another and another and another

I won't stop until I find at least one person to hold my hand

Enduring my loneliness until then

I Like

I like how you hold my hand and make me feel secure

I like how you push me out of the way

To the inside of the side walk without me noticing

I like how quick you are to open every door before me

Even how fast you are to get to my door before I am able to get out

Or I'm just always slow

(Smile)

I like how you think about the simplest thing before I even have a chance

I like how you let me go off and don't engage me

You know when to fight with me and fight for me

I like how you can calm my spirit with one look

One touch

One word

All at separate times using only one

I like how I feel protected with you

Guarding me better than the queen of England

Never do I have a want when I'm with you

When I'm not

You make sure everything is taken care of ahead of time

I like how we make decisions together

I trust you to do right just as you trust me to do right by you

I like how you tease me just to that look from me

I like how we play

I like how we love

I like how we are comfortable around each other

I like how you don't exclude me from things

But still give me the space and time to do me

I like you

I even love you

But I really just like you as a person

This is just a section

A piece of the grand "like" pie

I would like to tell you more but...

I like how you cater to me

Allowing me to cater to you as well

How you just give feet massages even when they are not freshly painted

How you love pleasing and pleasuring me

You're selfless

You only want my love for you

Sir

You have that and more

You can have whatever you like

Nothing is off limits that you need

08/22/12

I said I love you

You've made it very clear to me how you feel about me

By ignoring me

As I place a spread of emotions, words, and feelings

On a table of heart and soul

Just to watch you turn away from it like you never saw it at all

I said I loved you

More than you will ever know

To your back as you turned the other direction

Pursuing the next best and biggest thing

Presenting gifts as a sign of comradery

More thank you will ever know

Of the love I have for you

Time

Spaces

Reason

Seasons for pursing

This wall of love

I know not

What I do understand is that the

Reciprocity of my heart has turned away from me

Because of your lack of love for me

You are not ready

Fine

It's not our time

I get it

Tell me that upfront so that I know what hole not to throw my heart into

Even though I love you

Even miss you

Like crazy

It's even crazier for me to sit here

Believing that you have the capacity

To love me in return as I have loved you

Or maybe my love was not as pure as I first imagined

It was a shadow of my imagination

That I never allowed seeing the light of day

Maybe my hopes for us were just a secret

Locked in a bottle

Waiting to be uncorked

So you cold drink the richness of my wine

If I failed at my civil duty of exploring you and me

I do sincerely say I am sorry

It is

However

Yet and still

Not about me

But about you and the love I have

Had

And still do have for you

Naked, Alone, & Unafraid

Sadness creeps into remind me of how we are not we

I love you more than you will ever know

I guess I will just keep this between me and my journal

10/7/12

My mind keeps going back to him
How close I came to sleeping with him
It was to the point that I turned down
Certain activities and favors
Because I knew it would escalate
I saw how bad he wanted to do it
I could feel the pressure of him wanting to be with me
Inside me
All I could ask was
"Is this really happening?"
"Are you sure?"
He was sure
I was not
It did not happen
Logically it made no sense
Even though my heart, mind, and body wanted it
It would not have changed where we are
I don't know what pushed him
If it was my tears
Or just the part of him missing me
I still don't know all of him
What was I supposed to do?
Sleep with him?
The moral of the story is that I didn't

But I've gotten to the point where it was an option

Instead of a heart belief

I've walked into more situations that have led me to this place

Than ones that haven't

And I found myself loving him more than

Any man in my life before

There was about a 1% increase that I had in love for God

That 1% stopped me

I don't understand how or why

Because I keep getting into these situations

I almost wish this thorn would be removed from me

But it reminds me of that 1% love I have for God

1% more than whatever I'm dealing with

Each situation makes me want my desire less than the last

And want more of the fullness of God more

Yet I don't know how to reconcile the two

One constantly pulls at me

I question if my attitude or actions

Could separate me from who God has called me to be

At this point

I would need to be kept way from men period

To not desire them

To not desire the relationship

It runs very deep within me

And I don't know how to reconcile it

Did I love him or the thought of him?

What happens when I want to love someone again?

I keep being pulled back to God

No man has shown himself to be worth the effort of the sin

There were other sins but that ultimate intimacy where I know God

To invite someone that would change me and them

Because I am changed

Sex Addict

Love Addict

Attention starved

Maybe all

But 1% of me waits for the manifestation of the

Mustard seed of faith

For my husband

I never would or could make it this long with God

I loved him

But I love God more

10/22/12

To be happy and sad at the same time

Now fully aware of me and how I came across

I feel like its 2001 again

Where I am begging God to change me

Save me

Heal me

And I will be different

As I feel the tugs to just give up

Again

There is no turning back

The part of me that wants to is so small

I believe it is because of the belief

That I have to compete on the world's standards

Verse

The world compete against me

I have to lower myself all over again to fit in

But I don't fit

My frame won't let me squeeze into the holes of the crowded walls and spaces

My height makes me too tall

My weight makes me too heavy

When I come into the room

You have to make room for me

Not because of my physical weight

But the weight of the glory on my life

And me

12/07/12

Last night we went to sleep

It was a good night

Today we woke up

It was a good day

What a lifetime that has been lived

In a process of two weeks

Not one life has changed but two

I can totally see the parts of me

That surrendered to all of you

Giving up the fight that was so surely life long

Only to help a sister indeed

Who was a sister in need?

What a turn of events where I did nothing to have to repent

Know god's grace for the allotted space in my life

A rate of growth I would have never known

If it wasn't for the break in my life

03/07/13

I turned the other cheek

Until it was bruised purple blue

Knowing that no one can come to my rescue

For this is for my good

Why does it hurt so?

Am I bruised to the bone?

Will people always remember me?

The before me or the beaten me

Will the stain always come through?

That I was once black and blue

And no one came to my rescue

Since I choose this lot in life

And because I chose you

I must have been wrong

I know I was

I wanted to change

Because I don't want to feel this way again

To be such a disappointment

And a delight in the same hand

A coin of 50/50

Chance of what will be given

With so much knowledge and ignorance

In the same words

That was right on the money

Identifying problems in the mist of the situation

Utilizing the wisdom you've given

I was wrong

Timing, message, delivery, receiver

All wrong

How can it be that you have enlightened me only to shut me up?

How is that your will God?

That every other word is more damaging than encouraging

That the difference between me and an abuser is

Nothing

My only hope was to be used

Now my reality is to just watch and see

Pick up the trash

Clean up the scraps

Complete whatever tasks in front of me

Silently

No sense in creating a bigger mess

With my mouth than whatever is present

If you value my silence

Without words I will respond to you

And to others

For I don't want someone else

Broken for the lack of my ability to control my tongue

Silence it will be

I will tell my soul to scream

Because at least God will hear me

Candace Eldridge

03/18/13

Can I say that I loved him?

Yes I can

Was it like the love before?

I don't know

What I do know is that

Physically yearn for his closeness

I daydream about him at night

Wishing to run into him

Hoping that at the sight of me

He would remember

This love, this love

Should not be replaced

This love, this love

Left him lying awake

If you can feel me like you say you do

I leave this question for you

Do you love me?

Or did you ever

Because I know I loved you

Each change I make

A thought of you drifts though my mind

Looking for replacements

Never really finding

How much do I hold myself back from loving again?

I don't know
All I can do is hope that
This love, this love
Stands the test of time
This love, this love
Is real in this life
Forever in your memory
Never forgotten
Now I guess I can move forward
I've waited long enough
Hoping for your touch
His love is not yours
It is different and unique
But when he sees me
He never leaves
Because
This love, this love
Held his attention
This love, this love
Is never in remission
Is as steady as time
He walks towards me and welcomes me
He is mine

04/26/13

Why does disappointment hurt so bad?

Why do I even allow myself to be subject to these feelings?

As soon as I am able to handle the rejection

I will be ready for world domination

Because no one's opinion will matter

And I will have my freedom

Not being afraid of anyone or their opinions of me

Able to walk without the cares of the world

I am as I should be

Candace Eldridge

05/28/13

Trying so hard to get some where

Yet wondering why I can't stop and smell the flowers

Why there is not a pause

When the pause is there

Why is the pause not enough?

Constant grind and movement

Truth in desire to accomplish everything I possibly can

Candace Eldridge

11/20/13

Taking off the mask set in place for me to wear

Opening my eyes trying to focus

There is light and color

A breeze on my face

Blurriness

Uncertainty sets as the realization of things becoming clear

Hearts and minds wondering

I hear their disbelief

I blink once

I blink twice

A little more clear

The destiny set before me

The voices I now see

And fear

But I can't turn around now

Now way no how nowhere to go

The mask is not within reach

Breathing the breeze on my face

Was never so clear

So crisp

Panic setting in as focus becomes clear

Can't run backwards towards the guardedness of my heart

Now I'm all open

Wide

For all to see

"Get some courage" I tell myself

"Man up to the position"

Don't know left or right

Don't know right or wrong

But I'm here

Feeling my face and the dew of my sweat

Eyes seeing vibrant colors

Cool autumns, warm winters, flashy springs, summer all day long

Eyes twinkling with the spirit reborn

White teeth

White teeth all around me

A throat clears and I sit up straight

Suddenly conscious that they are waiting for me

They move when I move because they know not what to expect from this

Predicament

So I straighten up a little more

Back a bit taller

In - hole - in

Eyes wide open

And I speak...

"I'm ready now...

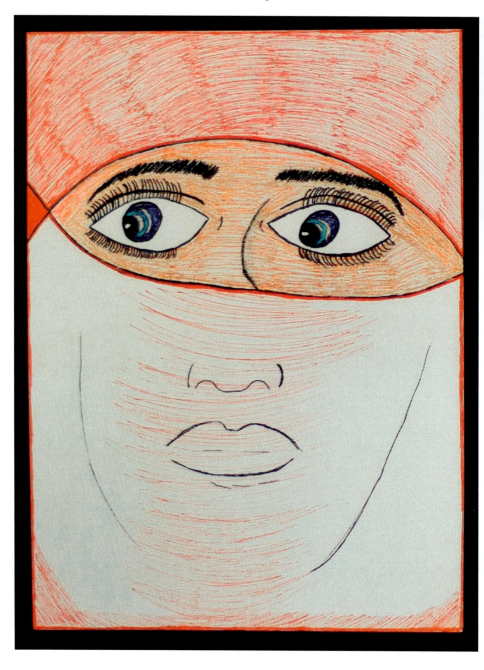

The Sky

The bluest horizon

Lined with clouds;

Freshness of the ocean

Far...

Wide...

Deep...

Reaching to touch yet never fully getting a hold of

Salty-sweet sweat on my lips

Causing me to be dehydrated and thirsting for more.

The smell of freshness, clean crisp air:

Warm to the touch and warm to the taste;

Refreshing life-giving like a glass of water

Most desirous of its attention and affection because with the blue sky comes an orange sun

Vibrating worth and fullness

Gaining the heat of life on my skin as it glows into a golden brown.

Wanting more and more attention like a long lost puppy

Sweat dripping

But satisfied

Crash

Blaring lights and horns all around

Glass shattered onto the street

Opening my eyes to see the ambulance and firefighters surrounding me

Many voices all asking for my attention

Trying to focus and trying to listen

The smell of oil combined with the smell of fear.

The taste of salt and dread upon my lips

Dry, dry lips yet I have no saliva to lick them

My mouth is dry and I'm grasping for air

Body is shuttering because of fear.

Questions popping in my mind 100 miles a minute

Who, what, where, when, and why how did this happen?

Tension in my body

Pressure in my head

Wanting to sleep but happy I'm not dead

Fingers and toes?

 Check.

Knees and hips?

Check.

Elbows and shoulders?

Check?

Neck and back?

Check.

Naked, Alone, & Unafraid

Breathe in and breathe out.

 Check.

All things are in alignment though everything is chaos around me.

Faces of concern, despair, and nonchalant

Their expressions are frightening me more than I actually feel.

Encouraging myself by saying, "I will be ok…"

Calming my soul like a summer breeze

Fading into a reality of peace

Dreams of tranquility shut out the noise around me.

No need to worry because I am here.

I will always be here.

Though you may fear,

There is nothing to fear.

Opening my eyes to see that the faces all around me look like me

Breathe in and breathe out

Voices are quiet now and all I hear are the breaths of my chest and the beep of the machine.

I rest…

Lily Pad

Rib bit! Rib bit! Rib bit!

I heard my prince say

As he leaped from lily pad to lily pad

Rib bit! Rib bit! Rib bit!

Is what I said

As I tasted the fried frog leg

Crispy and salty was the crust

The meat was tender like chicken

It smelled of grease and flour and the love of the kitchen

Southern, Cajun, and Creole

Naked, Alone, & Unafraid

Just right for me

Small in size

Gentle in frame

Yummy in my tummy

Satisfying my brain

Unending Pain... Or Is It?

How do you deal with a world full of devastation, trauma, hurt, and pain?
How can you turn a blind man's eye away from the canvas of blood and lost life?
Finding the joy in this trauma seems like an unrealistic request,
Yet to continue living even when someone else has not had the opportunity
Is required
The living God still lives
Even amongst the pain.
When did we stop caring about how our actions may affect others?
As well as change the course of our own lives? When you think you hurt one,
You are really hurting all.
Pain to something we all can relate to
Even when it's not directly our own
For if we care for ourselves,
There is something within us to care for someone else.
What you need to know
Is that someone else?
Cares for you too
Even when you don't feel it or see it at an exact moment,
There is someone who is praying for you
Who cares how you are doing

Naked, Alone, & Unafraid

Even desires to hear from you so that their day is brightened.

In your darkest place of despair

When you feel like no one understands and no one cares,

There is always someone there for you to rely on

Who will never leave you nor forsake you;

Who cries with you when you're hurt?

And dances with you when you're happy

How? My Questions for God....

How do I do something meaningful, fulfilling, and impactful? With multiple degrees yet still trying to find some type of opportunity?
How do I move forward?
These are the constant questions that come up in my mind.

Trying not to think small while acknowledging that only God can conquer it all

I am just looking for my piece of the puzzle in moving forward

It is just a small fraction of the entire entity of God as big as He is

Where does my meaning come from?

When does the help begin to manifest?

I realize I can do all things through Christ Jesus and that is it.

So do it Lord.

I can do it only through you.

I can do it only if You are with me.

Not separate

Not alone, but alongside of you.

How else can it happen?

My hand shakes at the fear, but I push myself forward in the direction I feel is best,

Only to see that I lead the way into a pit of un-satisfaction

Been there and done that.

Not I.

Oh no, Lord,

Not this time.

If you want it done,

You're going to have to do it.

I'm not leading the way with this charge.

My heart is for you, but I know not what direction to turn it to but to you.

And guess what?

I tried it my way to find out that it sucks;

I will not be doing that again.

I was waiting for signs from heaven to fall down like manna.

I pushed forward thinking this is the way that you are directing me

Even when I was angry

Dealing with everything I was dealing with.

Not this time.

You are God,

Not I.

It's not a plea; it's a fact.

Getting in my own way of trying to make something happen

Work just does not work,

So I'm done.

How else can it happen but by the mighty hand of God?

If waiting is the Lot that was rolled in my direction;

If I prayed for patience to solidify the need for me to change my own soul within me;

If I am as pleasing to you as You say I seem to be

I'm not moving.

Jacob had it right:

Not until you bless me.

I'm not moving

Until you move me.

I will remove all the websites, the blogs, the Facebook account, the twitters and YouTube's.

I will not interview myself in preparation for the interviews to come.

I will not go out seeking the acknowledgement of the light that you decided to shine on me so brightly only to be disappointed in the people who choose not to see me.

No, I'm done.

 Done

You are God.

God of Abraham, Isaac, Jacob, David, Deborah, John, Jonah, Jesus, Paul, Saul, James, Mary, Rehab, and all those other Cray, messed up, and desperate people.

I'm included in that number.

I'm stubborn.

You said I would never be in this place again;

You told that to the Israelites and to me, but I'm here.

No judgment upon you Lord;

I very well could have put myself back in this predicament by not listening to your direction

I am here now though, sir!

And I is not leaving until you bless me!

Put your hand on me!

Move the walls!

Bust down the door!

Blow down the windows!

I can't save the world!

But You can Save me....

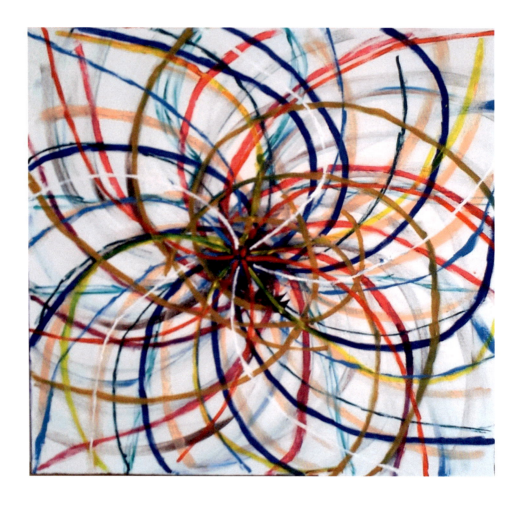

Too Easy

Do I fall easy?

Easier than most

But this boy got me topsy-turvy

A down home country boy

1 inch taller

4 shades darker

Juicy lips

And not at all thick

Do I know where he stands with Jesus?

No

But I know where he stands with me.

Just for him to be around is enough right now

To see him,

Get a whiff of his scent,

To put my finger out and touch him

A touch is enough to comfort me for the moment,

But it won't satisfy my soul.

However

In that moment I am lost.

It's like real right there.

For me to touch the soft, dark brown skin of his hand...

It's real.

I yearn for more;

I want to add another finger

Then two

I keep going until I have touched him with all five of my senses on fire -

I mean my fingers -

And we touch

But for a moment but that moment is enough.

He keeps doing what he does:

Washes my car

Armor oils my tires

Brings me milkshakes from McDonald's

Heck that's enough.

He acts like he's at home,

And I am where I am supposed to be,

At home,

Then he touches me

Ever and always so softly

I would do just about anything just for him to keep touching me softly.

That nice short massage on my shoulder

Or his head on my neck;

Him coming to be close to me

Whether it be besides me or in front of me;

And he touches me

Ever so softly and sweetly

I think I'm fine.

I'm just a junkie with a time limit

Because I know he will go... eventually.

But in that moment

He touched me.

He lays me down

Softly, slowly, sweetly

Just resting his head on my shoulder

Nudging his nose into my neck so that he can have the memory of my scent once again

We lay.

We just lay there

His breath on my neck and my hand on his back

And we just lay.

In my past life

This moment would have passed by differently

As he nestled into my neck and as I caressed his back...

Yeah it would have been different.

A door would have been opened with no return,

But we just lay

Ever so softly and sweetly

Though we are there for only a moment,

That moment being past,

It was enough to show me what I could not see

As we lay

There was an envelope of cover that came with that moment;

It was like he fit and I was enthralled to be

Covered by this immeasurable sheet that completely took me over for that moment

I grew tense

Not wanting to move.

Knowing me

There would have been a turn, an arching, and an arm

Wanting to move but not wanting to move.

I was covered with this sheet

And under it

There I was -

Tense, racing, running, overwhelmed, overcooked, over tested, and ready to blow.

I did not move

Instead I lay there

Letting my temperature rise

Waiting for an invitation but not wanting one to come.

The sheet that draped us was for but a moment

Just a moment was all that was needed.

As he rose to do him

I fell into my place of calm, peace, cooling.

Ooh... what a moment.

Not knowing the future

Not knowing his past

Just in the moment

Thank God for the moments that reminds me of me:

Oh so soft and sweet.

Naked, Alone, & Unafraid

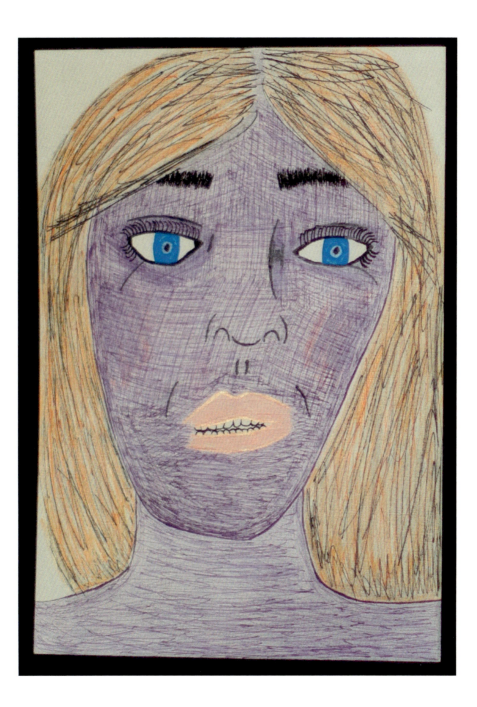

IJUSWANASING

Song penetrates my heart.

It's a separate beat -

Not abnormal nor a medical dysfunction,

But a beat from within

Someplace inside of me

There is a door with a window

With a hole

It was leaking.

How can this be?

I see the notes flowing sporadically.

They fell through the small hole of the window on the door

Hitting the floor

Making small puddles that come together forming a larger note

That then flows into the crack on the floor into the veins and tissue and blood that flows through me

To create a moment of creativity that presents itself in the form of a song

Or a spoken word poem.

Ijuswanasing

The music loud from the hills

From the hills of my heart

Where all its moments and/or seasons are being filled with lyrical beats

Running through the land like a living river

Flowing into new lands of harmony and love

Via rhythmic flowing form

Ijuswanasing

I never said I was Barry White, Barry Manilow, Brittany Spears,

Anita Baker, Chaka Chan, Guns & Roses, Meatloaf, Dido, Oprah,

Jamie Foxx, The Temptations, or The Five Heartbeats.

No, that is not me.

I have a natural, but I am not Jill Scott.

I got a big ole' booty, but I am not Shawna.

The music that flows inside of me has more to do with that feeling...

Off-chord

On-key

I will sing.

You don't have to buy my album.

I'm already a triple double with a cherry on top gold.

Ijustwannasing.

I just wanna let the music flow.

I just wanna sing.

Can't you feel my heart beat?

Off-chord

On-key

Ijuswannasing

I'm a Virgin

I'm a virgin.

I'm a virgin

Of many things but not enough

But for the purpose of focus

Let's say this stage…

This maybe my debut

My moment

My chance

My hope

Do I wish to be discovered?

Not so much as I wish to not suck.

It's my hope not to choke on the smoke of this lyrical content

Making a fool of me,

Wanting you to be pleased

And giving me real applause,

Real feedback, real props

On getting up on this stage

Of 1, 5, 10, 100, 1 million

To take my licking and keep on keeping on

I'm a virgin

Of this Mic… Is this the way to hold it right?

A way to breathe that fresh breath

Of air that you long to hear;

Not to sound the same

But enough difference to diversify

Myself from the audience

I'm a virgin of the world of spoken word

Classically trained in quick comebacks, smart remarks, and attitudes

flowing easily

My words on this stage

In this Mic will hopefully bring a better reflection of a girl

Stuck behind words

Never revealing herself

I'm a virgin

To this stage

This Mic

This life

They say the first step to recovery is admitting you have a problem.

Hi my name is Candace,

And I'm a virgin.

PS – it will get better.

Wanna Be, Wanna Be, Wanna Be Me

No one can decide my life but God

And me

If you're not one of those two people,

Don't make a decision about who you think I am; want me to be, or who I was.

I am none of those thoughts and yet I am all of them.

If my life were to be determined by the smallness of your thought process,

I wouldn't be here.

If I am ordained and chosen by God,

I am moved by God.

If I am chosen and moved by self,

I am moved by you.

You have no power, right, rhyme, or reason,

I know God moves.

I know God ordains.

I know God.

Not like perfectly but I have enough understanding to know when, where, how, why, and what not to do.

When I'm wrong, I go back to the beginning.

When you are wrong

You are just wrong.

How ironic?

I don't want to be anything other than what I've been trying to be lately.

I just wanna be me.

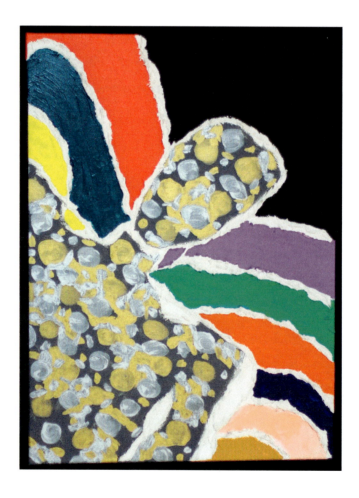

It's So Simple It's Hard...

It's so simple, it's hard...

Life

Love

Peace

Happiness

Prosperity

All the things of this world that are available at one's fingertips yet has been outside of arm's reach for one reason or another.

God, love, life, peace, hope, truth, trust

Words are just words yet they are also elements of the reality within reach.

It's so simple, it's hard...

To let go;

To live to realize that we can be what we dare to dream.

It's so hard yet so simple...

To let those who wish to transform the greatness of our destinies

Into simple childhood fantasies

Know

That my life is mine to live

You need to mind your own business because it's not yours;

That God destined my life to be mine for a reason.

I hear you, but I don't receive your negativity.

It's so hard...

To just love like it's the first piece of sweet candy ever to touch one's lips;
That all those things that come with the love has to be a reality open to being dealt with
The only secret thing between that love is between those sheets.
The good, the bad, the ugly, and the fun of love;
Not the fairy tale.
It's so simple...
God
Let Him do him and be in partnership with what He does.
Your life will be so much better.
It's so hard, it's simple...
I know that I can be whoever I want to be;
As large or small as my eyes can see
In the mirror of life before me
It's just a matter of me going through the process of life that my dreams will be... real.
It's so hard, it is simple:
Live Life... Seek Truth... Love God

The Introduction

So and so,

This is my friend Courtney.

Courtney,

This is so and so.

The look on my face shot through him like a bolt of lightning.

How could you stand there and introduce me as if I meant nothing to you?

What happened to those few moments before when you were holding me and kissing me trying to get every second with me before company came over?

What happened since last night?

What happened since a couple of days ago?

Almost two months ago?

Was that all a figment of my imagination that you allowed me to come up with this alternative reality because it suited your purposes?

What about my purpose?

My feelings?

You know what?

It's ok for you to have friends.

Let the best woman be the last one standing.

Not that I have anything against you so and so,

It's just that you happened to step into my territory or at least the territory I was about to claim as my own

But it's really not even you,

It's him!
You see my name's not Courtney, it's Candace!
He might as well have called your name out while we were in-between the sheets
Where I was allowing him to search my every crevice and cavity
Courtney!
Hold up, Shawty!
You're here telling me that after these past few months together you still don't know my name?
I met your family;
I introduced you to my friends;
You came to my church.
I finally get it:
It's not that I don't mean something to you because I do,
It's just that you haven't come into the understanding of the fullness of my glory.
You don't find me worthy enough to remember my name.
The time from then until now must not have impacted you as much as it did me.
I saw you,
I saw your worth.
I told God my motives were pure when I began to introduce myself to you.
Even when it made me feel less than equal or even loved,
You showed me that I placed your value over my own.

Well no more!
You are good!
And have been good to me!
But until you realize how precious I am and how much God loves me, you won't know me or see me
Because I don't want to say anything negative to you or about you cause words have power.
I will say this -
Since you don't know my name, which is ok
I have another one for you -
Meet my God.
Get to know Him because he is going to be that one to make a door in the desert for you to leave the dry land.
I love myself right now and I know my name.
Get to know God's then come holla at me!

My Prayer for Him

I would pray for the man which would be my husband
The one that would be all You created him to be just for me
Though I am still striving for the mark
He is not in the place to receive me
To be right to He and to me
I must uplift his needs to thee
How unfair of me to pray that
He be developed into the image of He
Which would be my male compliment?
To say that the potential of this man
Will be enough to grant him access to me
What about him?
And who he is to be?
So I say
Put my needs behind me
And put some extra of You into He
Let your love be enough for him to long for
Your light required to shine for his eyes to see
Not to make up for my lace of love and trust
Not to give up his livelihood just to be in mine
I need him not to see me
But to see Your love
That the only way to get to me is through You
I should not be a trophy to win

Just another running alongside him as a way of life
Trying to be more and better and happy and content
Whole in you
Which is the only way to be whole?
I pray for his salvation
I pray for his true joy to come through You
I pray that he not be moved by the physical world
But start moving from the spirit
I pray for your power to overshadow all the bad
When that man looks in the mirror
He sees You
You have equipped him with love and kindness
With the ability to love in a way so genuine
He walks in authority though he knows not
Where it comes form

You Ain't the One

You walked in the door

And everything about you said something wrong

I walked toward you to kiss you

To tell you I missed you

I never reached you because you were gone again

So I followed you down the hall

Where you started questioning me

"Where you been?"

"Why didn't you call?"

"I've been working hard baby, same thing every day."

I touched your arm and you pulled away

This type of coldness in ever felt before

But baby, why are you worrying?

I would never betray our love...

As the door slammed

Time stood still

Those birthdays, each holiday, and anniversaries

Family gatherings

All for what?

To have this door slammed in my face?

Oh Lord

Oh Lord

Oh Lord

Oh Lord

It was silent... quiet

I'm glad I know now before I just accepted you for who you are

You ain't the one

I deserve better

Naked, Alone, & Unafraid

A Love Letter to My Daddy

How blessed you are Lord of Hosts

How blessed I am to be loved by you

The impressions you have left on me is visible for the world to see

Your embraces last throughout the night

I am warm in your embrace

Because we are surrounded by hosts of angels

I don't mind an audience

They just went to be close to you as well

This love is real Lord Jesus

It changes every place I came to

It sets every crooked way straight

I am embraced and embracing your long arms of righteousness

I won't let go

Not even I the morning so that you can go to work

I won't change this love in my heart unless you tell me to

If it shuts people out

Tell me to crack a door to let them in

Otherwise they will just be left out

I'm greedy

I'm stubborn

I'm not sharing

You said what is mine is mine and you are mine Lord

I am no the smallest, tallest, prettiest, smartest, quietest

Rich or poorest but I still not letting go

At least for the moment

I will share

I will

Eventually

I know more people need to feel your glory

But....

To be enclosed in a dark room with the door shut I turn on the lights because I want to see your face

The fullness of your grace to abound upon me making me chase you for more because this feeling in my soul forces me to get my next hit off you and your glory

I want to exhale again

Falling into the abyss of your strong arms

Allowing myself to fall again and again and again

And again

Into

Holy

Love

We are a Reflection of Your Perfection.

We are a reflection of your perfection.

A mirror image of your goodness on the earth

A clear representation of your glory

One who is a small piece of your overall body

Too small for you to take notice

Yet still you know my name.

I appreciate the fact that you cannot see my shortcomings

Only a reflection of the truth and depth of your love

I am good with the fact that

My human representation is misunderstood and judged

For they might not see the beauty of your majesty

Oh God

All of my scars and bruises are highlighted

The weight of the burdens and hurts

Add to my frame and size

Modern day beauty is not beauty in your eyes

The spiritual lens that only sees

Speckles of light

Brilliant colors representing your characteristics

Love

Holiness

Joy

Justice

Kindness

Peace

Might

Shining onto the reflection of the mirror

To the point that you cannot even see anymore

Too bright for the human eyes to take

The magnificence of the sun where man shields his eyes

But I look into your face

And see your glory

Never ashamed of the reflection looking back at me

Perspective

Perspective
Depicting volumes and spatial relationships on a flat surface
Relating to space
Relationships
Unlimited in which all things occur or are located
Space in proportion to the extent or room given
In a relationship
This is supposed to be our connection
Between two people that is either by blood or marriage
We are neither
Just a couple of people with what was an emotional connection
Yet may have been something completely different
A relationship going through the process of growth and formation
Sometimes growing together
Sometimes growing apart though not forever

The Hardest Part

The hardest part about being honest is being honest
The honesty I'm thinking in my head is different from what I would actually say
My current honesty is misleading to be the whole truth of my heart
Not the case
My heart is currently in prison in my body being locked up for no one to hurt
I've been careless with my heart
I asked without praying
I engaged instead of ministering by walking away
I lied that I liked what you did or said to make sure my loveliness quota was never reached
I accommodated behaviors and treatments because I know the abuses of life better than the love
I take self-responsibility for my participation in these actions
I am not choosing God
like never before
Though it appeared that I always did
I am no longer putting humanity before divinity
Nor my sanity after your acceptance
I honestly don't want it in my life anymore
Not because there is something wrong with you
I am just figuring out what is right for me
My health and sanity

My heart broken not shattered

In to miniature puzzle pieces that can only be pieced together by my prince of peace

Really, I love you

Sometimes I love you

And want the best for you

More than I wanted it for myself

That is a conclusion I dare not reach

For the sorrows of life try to swallow me up whole

Like my name is Jonah

Disillusioned by sadness of yet another relational failure

Failing to meet the requirements of life as well as fulfilling

Running on the hamster mill like Love and Hip Hop or Housewives of Whatever

I can't put you first in an inauthentic relationship

Where I ignore all the warning signs just to have a moment of your time

That is not truth

That is not love

It is two people not caring enough

For themselves to let go

I applaud you in taking the first step

Hurting like heck

Seeing the necessity of the actions as God's way to get my drastic attention

I don't blame you so don't be mad at me

Just trying to express myself while not in my feelings

Forcing me to run after God even more to fill the void

Careful not to exhaust my hurts only for them to be replaced

This time alone is good

It is what I need

I accept this position in life

Not punishment but growth

Choosing God above all others

Guiding me along the way

Have faith

He has you too

No worries

I still love you

But I release you to do you

1:58 PM

There was a mention of sadness in my eyes

And it is true

It goes with the demise of what is happening between me and you

I still smile for I know it is alright

And it will be alright too

No denying my feelings every time I see you

Swelling my pride

Take the hurt and pain

Back to the empty place inside

It will be alright, and it already is

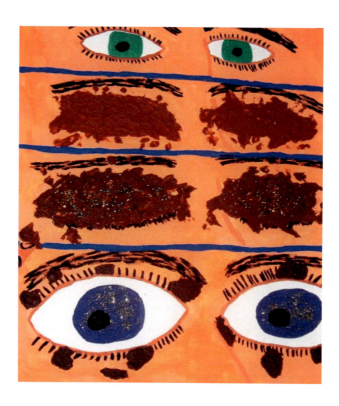

Purpose Pusher – THANKS!!

The demise of this relationship is like a living death

Deaths where I can see you move, have your being, and take another breath

All the while

I am watching with hurt and sorrow

I breathe I the life we had together

I breathe out an exhale signifying our separation

It wasn't like we were breathing the same breath

If we were

My inhale would be exhaled out of your lungs

No, we are living as two separate entities

Equal in tax status

Uneven in rank

I think the worst part is me thinking there was more here than I could see

To see you pulling away with a reason or cause

Checking to see if I did something wrong

Only to see the look in your eyes that you despise me

Even while you love me

I find it amazing how close love and hate is

I love you, but I hate how you are treating me

I love you, but you love him and her differently

Than you love me

My shrinking no longer allowed as my room only got smaller and smaller

When I went to stretch my legs

I busted through the door into your space

Not to push you out on purpose

There just wasn't any other place for me to grow

I had to make a decision about moving on

Hurting me yet not realizing I was sealing the coffin on the relationship

How unaware I have been with my eyes wide open shut

So funny to think back on how I wanted you to be in my wedding

Yet you wanted to be in another state

So funny that I tried to include you and you ran

I thought it was me but it was you the whole time

I despise your revelation though it is pushing me to my purpose

I can no longer stay in your comfortable place

I have to move on

Since you say it was never me

Sometimes relationships fall apart

I wish you happiness and health

Wealth and a good heart

Good luck on your new adventure in life

I am sure you will do fine

But I am done and moving on

I just don't have time

To contemplate

What

How

Why

And when

Do you

I am doing me

I am going to win

My life is not my own

Nor is yours

Thanks for pushing me towards my purpose

Consider this your reward

Mas Y Mas

More and more I am realizing the reasons and seasons of things
Life is not supposed to be singularly lived
But interwoven into a garment of intention
Beautiful to some and a waste to others
The end product one of long-lasting elasticity and bear-ability
Caressing the skin of those who came after the work is done
Trying to provide shelter and protection against the elements of life already experienced
Each piece of thread representing growth
Growing through pain
Growing through sorrow and mourning
Growing through being stretched so thin that you thought you would break
Yet you were combined with other threads just to strengthen you

You Make Me Brave

You make me brave

You make me brave

You make me brave

You make me brave

Even though I want you to come over

I want you to want me more

Want me to the point that you express words of hope

About us

Where you don't me wonder

Where my waiting is justified

My needs are addressed above your desires

In you I can lose myself

Having done so before

Making accommodations to fill the moment

No lasting effects come into play since I let you play no more

It's difficult

Hard

But I have to love me now

Waiting for you to care at the level of my need

Is an impossible feat

I have too much hurt and brokenness that your hugs can not fix

If you allow me to use you

I will

But I don't want to

You are special to me

You are a man of God and a child of God

It is best for me to leave you be

So God can determine and teach you who you are

I can make accommodations, but that would be like

Me swallowing globs of vomit of food I just can't get down

Thank you for your hugs

They helped heal me at the worst time

But I gotta do me and you do you

As I partner with God

You partner with God

Maybe God will allow me to partner with you

If not

I am sure someone is waiting on that dance

I know God is the best partner you can ever have

Love Who I Love and Hate Who I Hate

I am a black woman

And a Christian

I am an angry black woman

Not for the reasons media has portrayed me to be

I am mad

Because of the position of the world

The uncompromising message has to present

As a black woman who is a Christian

It may be easy for you to take judgement out on the wrong doers

The one who harass our children for being black

Killing them as adults because they are black

Threatened by their blackness

Because they are black

A cycle that would seem to end with the progression of a black president

The systems maintain modern day slavery

Today American blacks are still considered slaves

Do you know what slavery is?

It is

One

Being forced to work through mental or physical threat

But that is why workers-man comp was created right?

Two

Being owned or controlled by an 'employer'

Usually through mental or physical abuse or the threat of abuse

Oh, Hello sex slaves

Three

Being dehumanized

Treated as a commodity or bought and sold as property

Welcome to the NFL, NBA, or MLB

Or meeting any cops on the street stopping people with no real justified reason

Four

Being physically constrained or having restrictions placed on his or her freedom of movement

Freedom of movement

Lawfully having the right to move inside a state and outside

The right to the liberty of movement

The freedom to choose one's residence

According to the universal declaration of human rights

This is true

Until my or another black person's movement inconveniences you

Right?

Trayvon Martin

Black teenage girl at the pool party in Texas

But is ok

I forgive you

I must look beyond my self-identity though I really don't know how

Or what I might be

To look at humanity from a God who loves everybody

Don't get it twisted

God loves everybody

For every life wrongfully taken

The earth cries out

Yet God also forgives those who ask for forgiveness

And Repents

God is angry with our sins

It is not a "God made me sin" kind thing

But A

"I have decided to take my own life and the life of others into my own hands"

The sin that says

"It is now my responsibility to do racial cleansing"

Dominican Republic

"I must protect this country at all costs" sin

Dylan Roof or ISIS or Al Quada

I don't remember

I'm not angry and I forgive you

I'm not angry because God love me

I'm not mad because God is a God of justice

Yeah Right!!!

The only reason I write as a form of art is because the Lord says

Vengeance is His and His alone

And every time I think of the senseless losses

Of those who look like me

Or not like me but who I racially identify with

Vengeance arises

Maybe its hurt and pain for the continual loss of a people

If it wasn't so mainstream

I don't know if I would be so affected

06/28/15

I never thought my life would turn out like this

Following God's lead

As He dismantles every part of me

And my life

I think that was my problem

The lack of imagination

I thought married, babies, executive job in a high rise, soccer, YMCA, kids church, super fine and hot, successful husband

Family and friends

You see

 I did what I was supposed to do

A good student and athlete in high school

Full extracurricular activities

Successful college career

Followed the Lord's call to move where no family was

Grad school

Grad School again

Still following God's leading

Broke his heart

While this other one broke mine

Friendships started and ended

Hurt and misunderstanding

Still following God

Naked, Alone, & Unafraid

I never thought about my life I this way

That is my mistake

Taking my life into my own hands

Instead of releasing my plans into Your hands Lord

Allowing for the desires of my heart

To lead me to an unknown land amongst a people I was too afraid to engage for fear they may truly understand me

Lived in the reality of a doomed determination of unhappiness and accommodating

Me making accommodations to fit into a space

Where I am too awkward to fit

"Me"

I know who I am.

I know what I got.

I know what to put in this back pocket to make it pop.

Exactly

My skin so soft and sweet

That's why they call me Candy

Because I always bring a sweet taste to whatever I speak.

Sometimes I'm toffee

Other times Laffy-Taffy,

Then I'm chocolate covered pretzels.

You can have that salty-sweet.

I know who I am.

I know who I be.

I walk with authority.

Forget walking softly;

I walk loud.

I want you to know I'm coming

With a vengeance and a swiftness that just rolls up on you and you don't know what to do because I speak and I'm in front of you.

Boo!

HA HA HA!

I know who I am, but you don't know who you are

Wandering around from place to place and town to town

Looking for a home

Looking to fit in

Realizing and still dealing with these people

Who you and I know are not your friends.

I know who I am,

But you don't know me.

You don't realize that the vessel you see

Is a vessel created, manufactured and distributed by the one and only J.E.S.U.S.

That I was made in His image so I'm really just imagery:

A figment of your imagination, transparent as wax paper

You see, I know who I am and who sent me:

The one and only king of kings, Lord of Lords, Prince of Peace

And He made me ... me.

I know who I am so let me introduce myself to you.

I am from a long lineage of Queens who ruled Ethiopia

Leading a kingdom and a country to prosperity, freedom, Jesus...

Before the haters came in destroying every living legacy or evidence of our existence

Stealing our dream, ideas, identities,

But I'm still here.

HAA HAA HAA!

I am built for stability from my thighs to my feet;

From my waist to my chest;

From my head to my shoulders

My loins birth out the life that lifetimes get to see and participate in if you're willing.

My back can hold down 1000 cans if they wanted to.

With a pretty face and small waist, I'm poison.

With my weapons of mass destruction

I can rule or reign;

Take lives or give them;

Set free and bind.

I AM ROYALTY

I can run the streets with the folks

Building a crew of monumental proportion

Or take it to Corp and bark at board members.

I am a kaleidoscope

Presenting the brilliant and colors of the world

You look at me and think I'm black, but my bloodline transcends thee;

I am part you and you and you and you.

I am related to the streets

I am related to and blended to one

So that I walk in with East Indians, Africans, American Indian, Mexican, Pilipino, Asian, White, Creole, and Caucasian

And you can't even tell the difference.

Jesus' hair was like wool and mine is like silk

It will get nappy on you if you let it.

I got the personality of the streets:

Buckhead to west end,

Florin to Antioch,

Arlington to Garland,

All those cities in-between and surrounding

You look at me, but you still don't know me.

You can get this understanding;

Ima' make this short and sweet -

I am walking the streets with my piece;

If you step to me, I might wet ya.

I keep going like the energizer bunny looking for opportunities to overcome and take over.

You either gonna roll with me or leave

Because I've declared this my block now my territory

Step and see.

I am a poet.

Yeah, I can rap and sing,

But you need to hear me talk to you

So that the truth remains

I am an artist learning to close my eyes and let my hands flow free

Creating depictions of beauty because there is nothing on this earth that's not clean

I am a philosopher.

Not Jung or Socrates,

But one of the streets making things comes together for everyone to understand and relate to.

I am a sister of the world.

We are separate and equal.

What you called trifling I call into holy being and mine trumps yours.

I am a mother of dreams, - some mine, some deferred -

Walking trying to figure out if this is mine to start or pass on.

I delegate responsibilities to the responsible one.

I am sensitive.

I see you when you cry;

I feel your pain.

I can't explain, but I understand.

You thought you knew me but you had no idea the reality that I spit is oh, so real.

Turning heads

Turning tables

Making something out of nothing

I create the atmosphere because I'm open to see what He will do through me.

I can go to the club or studio;

The playhouse or playground;

Underground or midtown

Infiltrating atmospheres that are not yours to keep

You thought that I came to spit at you, but this entire time I've been praying over you

That your spirit would be receptive to the

Living Spirit of God that gives;

For you to have peace in your circumstances;

For you to be willing to give

A piece of your mind for this one moment of time

Dreaming and thinking of those impossible dreams

Naked, Alone, & Unafraid

Ahh.... I see you and feel you.

It is alive.

It's alive in me too.

You see, I'm a vessel for the eternal God.

I am a gangster extending my squad

Ready to fight at a moment's notice

I am an artist trying to reach you intellectuals.

I am a queen leading a nation just like me

Representing God to the fullest and you didn't even see it until you suddenly changed.

I came into your sphere and caused you to change

Because that is what catalysts do

We rep for Him while working on you

I am Holy and pure,

Not a virgin but still anointed and trusted by Him

To reach the mass for heaven's sake

I know what some of you are thinking.

The nerve of me standing here preaching to you

The nerve!

But for those faithful few

I came for you

Meet me outside and we can chat.

I know who I am,

Do you?

The Thought

For you to think I don't think of you really pisses me off.

Like you are in the back of my mind,

The furthest point of consciousness,

A dream that reality has played with,

A diss

Like I don't value what we have,

Dream of what could be,

Cease to cease reality of there being an you and me.

A doubt

That my affection is true,

That I wouldn't walk to the ends of the earth to find you,

Or wait all these years

To give you the piece of my soul,

That only god knows.

It not easy

It's not supposed to be.

Stop thinking I wouldn't do what it takes

To keep you beside me if that's where

God wants you to be.

Can I give you my heart without you asking?

Must you instruct and dictate our every move?

Why must everything rest and depend on you?

What about me?

My thoughts, hopes, and dreams?

You are not the only one with thoughts.

I think of lying down with you and never wanting to get up,

Of all the dates and people I missed

Because I decided you were it.

Am I safe in your arms?

Would you betray me if I got close?

Or try to push me away because my scent

Reminds you of something or someone you are trying to forget?

I need to –

I want to teach you too.

And trust

There are things for you to learn,

But I made my decision.

Will there be a flow in this?

At this point a flow is all we have.

The 24, 48, 72, 96 hours does not replace the thousands of minutes apart.

I want to keep you while not losing me in the process

Because it's me I come home to

Alone

Don't sit here and doubt me.

Talk to me

Tell me your heart;

I want to hear it.

Just know that I'm not that second thought,

I'm the first one.

Naked, Alone, & Unafraid

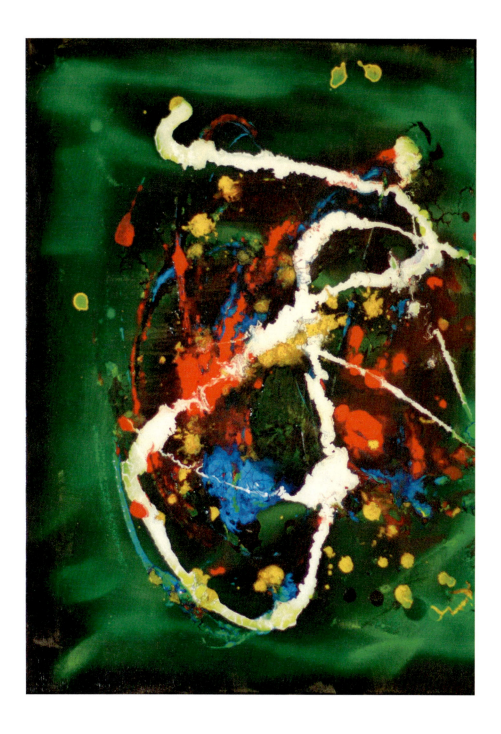

Life's Too Short

80 isn't young anymore,

It's closer to the end than we hoped for.

Watching life pass me by

Thinking tomorrow will always come

Bringing new life,

A new day,

New breath

Life's too short for bullshit -

Thinking everything is everything and the world revolves around me.

It is moving in circles and so are we

Looking for meaning, hope, peace, and being

The Treasure of a Woman's Heart

The hardest thing a man could do

Is to take possession of the treasure within a woman's heart

Don't think I can't see you squirming in these spot lights fellas

For some women, the booty isn't an issue

For others, it is the over opinionated personality

Yet the true treasure is not a thing but a person

You cannot receive it with a kiss

Nor with ears wide open shut

It has to be learned and caressed and cared for and cherished

The treasure of her heart

You see, that is the vulnerable place

The place of the deepest intimacy and personality

It is the place of comfort that makes each woman's distinct personality shine

The heart

It is where she moves and breathes

It is the part of her that others can only encourage but never fully engage unless permission is given

The heart of a woman is like

A rare almost extinct jewel

It must be handled with care

Transported with enough covering to guarantee it won't break

Even then, guarded by day and night

Her heart must be heard and felt to gain a little understanding

As the woman goes forward into more confidence of herself

Her heart shines brighter out of her eyes

Even with the men she loves,

She learns to unveil herself within his embrace

Just at the excitement of being seen

A woman is a jewel and her heart is the rarest peace

Not give me a piece but peace be still

Stiller than the cold echo of the winter's air

Peace

So gargantuan that only God can see and fill the space of time and gravity

As the world swims around the island of her joy

Love so immense that her blood flow drowns you

Fellas

You either sink or swim in the life she is giving you

Not her mind, body, or soul

But her heart

The place where only the deep swim

For those who can't are soon rescued into the lifeboat of exit

Exiting her heart is exiting her body never to be returned

Just like a new born baby

Please be gentle

Please be kind

If you are not the one to be the caretaker of her heart

Grab the lifeline

For she knows no hurt as the one who abuses the seas of the water of her personality

Her heart

 Let it shine

Where Do I End & You Begin?

I'm not a gusher

I don't get excited about babies or weddings

I will celebrate with you in that moment but I'm not a gusher

I like love

Actually, I love love

The thought of love sends butterflies flying into my heart

My stomach is settled now, and my heart is flying

But real love

Not vampires attracted to sweet blood

Not made in Manhattan

Not even you've got mail

Not Boyz in the Hood or Love Jones

All these don't give me the picture I am seeking

Maybe a little of Love and Basketball, Jason's Lyric

The love not the drama and the preacher's wife

The things that show longevity

That is love

The decision and declaration that forever is not long enough

I will always do my best for today

No fantasy but reality of love

In that way I'm a gusher

Barbie dolls were never my thing

Unless they were doing something nasty

I liked being outdoors, around people, and smelling dirt

Yeah I got my nails done but that didn't stop me from playing too

I like being physical

Pushing my body because I know the foundation of my bones is strong

I was build Tonka tough with a ford frame and Harley engineers rolling on 22's

Vibrant colors with a hemi engine

I know I'm bad

I'm vulnerable and sensitive

More sensitive than most

I give until I have nothing more to give

Then I give some more

Each age I learn more

Of what it means to say no

That it is ok

That caring for me is important too

As important if not more than what I do

If I give and never take any time for me, what am I left with?

Nothing but me

So, it's not selfish for me to care for me and think of me when others won't

Love Takes Time

Love takes time
There is no way for it to be rushed
Met at 22 for the first time again since 12
Though it was only a moment they were apart
Separation grew them into more
Then expected
Not knowing what to expect
Their moments are fast together
All regions of their being together
Until time separated them
To continue to learn the lessons the Master has in place for them
22 turns to 29
Evidence of needing self love overwhelms the need for space fillers
When seen again, though in different places
The memory of love overwhelms both
Truth of life separates them and a memory keeps them together
Until time no longer permits as well as lifestyle
32 rolls around and it still looks
Different than 22
A love lost was never the love that was supposed to be
It took that moment for both
To see that what they thought they were missing never was
Love really separates and brings back together again
Not in the original form but better

Naked, Alone, & Unafraid

Not together but still together

Love took time to grow within each one as they learned to love where they are

In their own skin

That love took time regardless of who was around them

Who they dated and who they ended up with

Love takes time

All the Fake Accolades...

Just as I was getting excited

Feeling the meaning behind your texts

Actions fell short of manhood

All the while you want to put an X on my chest

With claims of a grander life

Or at least more excitement

Yes I am included

Me and all your other wives

For you only have your prowess to show

Sexual stamina beyond the ages

All the tricks, bags, dimes, and books

Reach one teach one

Strengthening relationships

All the while you look like a crook

Where is your credentials?

Acknowledgement that you are legit

Naw...

You just a mudslinger

Throwing around some good dick

I left your pay on the night stand

Even left you a good tip

With all your dreams and aspirations

All you are offering is some good dick

The Man

I like a college educated man with street credibility

One that went to Harvard University

For a business degree

Yet keeps his childhood friends for grounding

I like a brother who can get down with the get down

While at the same time holding me down

He doesn't want Suzy or Rebecca

But a thick sistah with some weight on the back

"Girl, you light as a feather."

He says as he puts me over his shoulder

He is not ashamed of my size or my attitude

It excites him and keeps him engaged

Keeping it clean in the streets

Success is all he meets

Boardwalk to Boardroom Empire

Swagger never expires

Able to contemplate life with the leaders of the free world

Then going back to provide a hand to his fallen brother

His heritage runs brown beyond the rice fields of the Carolinas

West Africa he represents proudly

Never forgetting the lessons and sacrifices placed before him

Bleed truth like a leech

Refusing to let go of any knowledge he gained

For that is his liberty

It makes his freedom bell ring

Truth is he is a hustler

He will never work for the man again

He does what he has to do

Just to free his brother from chains

He went back again and again to get them

Will they ever change?

It doesn't matter

He will keep learning and letting his freedom ring

Obtaining the most prize possession of the race

The ability to learn the message of the race

So he can train the jockeys of the race

To control their horse and just win

Coming from behind

#10

The Black Man

Inside Out

Staring at my empty room

Full of possessions

Empty of persons

Wondering will the clock ever

Strike my name

My fortune, my fame

Fulfillment missing

Searching like a drug addict looking for my next hit

Consumed by the images outside my window

Wondering if it would ever be me

Walls to door frames

Windows to ceilings

Searching all over just to find a bit of meaning

Opening the garage door

While it is securely closed

There is no leaving

Only remaining in this home

Hearing a crackle I turn to the left

Fire blazing bright upon my canvas

I reach out my hand to gauge

Whether I am hallucinating or having a bad drug reaction

Warmth feeling the room

My hand, my blood

Desire creeping out of me to gain

More of the warmth

No opportunity

The flame is gone

Guiding my pencil

Whistling of papers

Throwing of ink

Spilling of paint

Trying to capture such incredible beauty

Yet all I see is an image of incomplete

Not good enough

Needing change and to be better

When I hear a knock on my garage window

"I saw the flame in my dream.

I just had to come and see.

It is true.

You captured the beauty."

I looked over to my left

Hearing the whistle again

Feeling the wind on my skin

Looking out

Only to look in

Everything I ever wanted or needed was already here

I don't have to go outside

I think I will stay in

Missing You So Much

Tried to change my heart

To make other people fill your space

I couldn't pass the test

Even in taking my emotion away

All that was left was my body and soul

This was not to be controlled

Missing the kiss for a lifetime

Where I would drift into outer space

Your willingness to share my space

Lets me know you will never be replaced

Time clicking by

As the sound of the train drawing near

Anxiety arising within me

Out of the fear you wouldn't take this journey with me

The horn or the train snaps me back

Boarding without you but my heart never leaves you

Missing the ...

Sun and cool breeze on my face

Kissing the life back into my soul

My reality is with you

It took you too long to get here so I'm never leaving you

I love you

Colors of Blood

"You are my starship

Take me up tonight and don't be late"

"Share my life (Share my life girl)

Your all I want (Trust in me girl)"

A touch could be a simple one

A kiss

A pat on the back

Caress of the hand

Love turns a simple touch into an adrenaline rush that pulse from the heart to every moving member of life

The power of love is very simple

When it comes together in the building stage

All parties participate in a growth plan that seems to follow the trends of life

When life come together in fragments

The pieces that are missing will either grow into the empty spaces

Or they will grow onto other areas already present

"I love you in a place where there is no space or time"

Equates to the feeling of completeness

Whether love is whole received or not

The position of love moves the least to the greatest

The only issue with love is that it is equated to romance

Love is so simple

It is the air that we breathe

Whether smog filled or ocean free

To inhale is love

Movement is love

Walking

Standing

Talking

Writing

Listening

Are all symbols of love?

The requirement of another person is based upon the requestor

The objectivity of love is beyond the normal

Denominator encompassing a number outside the framework of a working adult

But a child gets it

They know by a look whether love is received

Love is a song

"Our day will come"

Speckles of color within the fragments of blood

Dissected into palatable pieces

To be researched and documented

Conceptualize

She said to conceptualize

But I can't even capitalize the moment

She said to let go and do something different

How am I supposed to let go?

Thinking of life with you at this moment in time

Is harder than seeing the vision of us on the beach making love

Day to day breathe and release

Yet years from now I see total bliss

Unreal and unlike any other love I've known

You have answered so many prayers

It scares me to think what would happen

If I was all the way in

I want to spend time with you

Make wine with you

Spit a couple of rhymes with you but I can't

Hidden away by my fears that say they will betray my feelings in broad day light

Haunted by the notion that a token of your live is a s simple as a kiss

I tried you which means I tried something different

All the while knowing that I've never trusted my feelings

Not even a little bit

It is funny how the doctor said to just let go and live

All the while your message was mirrored through another person

Pray tell Lord?

Are you speaking?

Because I hear a voice and I want to make sure it is you...

Your servant is listening

You are so good to me and good for me I cannot lie

You feel me when I'm not with you

Yet when I'm close

My heart runs through my hands

Pulsating at a rhythm not known to man

Feeling every ping of nervousness because what you say is true

Watching your actions speaking louder than any

"I Love You"

In a flux and funk of emotions

So tied up in a swell

Of liberation and libations balled together

In a knot of hopelessness of my old self

The new me needs to be pinched

Just to make sure you are real

I am down for what you are cooking

Sushi anyone?

In or Out

I could use a double double animal style

But I would only be something to satisfy for the moment

Not fill the void or holes left open by uncertainty

What if you said yes?

What I be enough for you?

Could I compete with all the other?

Chick-a-dees who VI for your attention

With their younger, stylish, and sexually liberal ways

Do I fulfill a need that you have?

To grow together

Am I as I am enough?

What if you said no?

Saturated

Consumed with the much of life

Extending an olive branch to anyone who would listen

Or would buy

Taken over by aliens from another nature

Another world

Who doesn't want a home?

Just to take over yours

How did we let ourselves get here?

Lost in the rush

For gold

For souls

For money

For luck

The heart of the hoping

The joy of the lost

Just to make a dollar

Defiling the integrity of the referral

Modern day conversation

Strength and power of the human touch

Need for real life people and real life community

Will we be able to keep the early morning?

Meetings of my grandfather and his friends

At the local waffle house

Or will house touch be lost

Naked, Alone, & Unafraid

Like the next big sales pitch

Let the poser tell you what's hot

Instead of the air you breathe

Technology will connect you to humanity

Verses going to see your neighbor in person

Counting lights like they are the starts at night

I hope not to lose my sense of humanity

To the realness of the world

The Blame Game

I miss you so much though it is by my own hand
That you are not here with me
This is the blame Me game
Since I didn't do what you wanted
Make my hair how you like
Or my hips and waist to be that right size
I blame me for this loneliness I feel inside
But what about you
Only complimenting me because you like what you see
The moment you don't
You are judging me
This is the blame You game
Not feeling good enough
Or pretty enough
Or sexy enough to please you
Focused on my improvement potential
Verses
How I can help improve you
I blame you for this loneliness I feel inside
The trombone of my heart is snaring loudly
The rims of my soul is beating
Apart of my spirit died
When
I felt your breath leave my neck

Naked, Alone, & Unafraid

This is the blame we game

I blame the two of us for not making it work

I was stupid

You were dumb

And now we are both just hurt

Baby if you can forgive me

Let's try again

No more pointing fingers

Just holding hands

Blameless

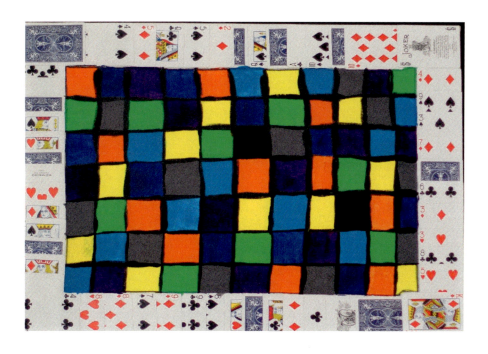

I still believe

I still believe

The impossible is possible

I still believe

What you said is true

I still believe

That dreams can become reality

I still believe

In you

Mountains and valleys

No one knows your thoughts

In the millions of particles of sand

No one of us can understand

Unless you breathe the word

Until you light the flame

Until the rocks cry out

Tomorrow, today, and yesterday the same

You did it before

And you will do it again

You did it before

I tell my soul

You did it before

And you will do it again

You did it before

I tell my soul

I still believe

Jesus

I still believe

God

I still believe

Holy Spirit

You will do it again

Speaking Silently

AAAAAAHHHHHHHHHHHHHHH

Typical again

I open my mouth to scream

At something

Somebody

And nothing comes out

I look you in your eyes

I see your stance

Know the thoughts that run

Through your head

Because I

See your soul

To know that I know you know

Truth without ceasing

I open my mouth

Nothing comes out yet I'm screaming

At you

Masturbating to the rhythm of a heartbeat

Fantasizing about the denseness of the fog you see

Blinding the eyes were not truth can be seen

Hoping for stupidity to lead me

Down the path of lacking understanding

And self-love

AAAAHHHHHH

I'm screaming at you

Silence speaking loudly

Words developing into

Shims, tions, ly, ing

Over and over

Louder and louder

Deeper trying to touch my deep

But you don't see me

Can't touch me

Boom!

Loud as can be

Your ear drums are racing trying

To piece back together

Every piece that I just shattered

BOOM!!

Displacing the logic you had

Boom! BoOm! BOOM!

My words are speaking

Muse

I forgot how much creative energy

Flow when I just let it

How the depths of my love is now measured from

The bottom of the sea floor

To the heights of heavenly

How my opportunities suddenly became possibilities and then realities

How?

When I let go

My juices flow

Darkness of the realities of life surrounded me

Created the sight of the blind within me

Pits of despair like inception

Each level taking a greater dedication

Rivers running intensely

Penetrating profoundness unseen

Unless it's too deep

Into my no where's is where you found me

Resuscitating volumes of life into

My dry veins

In my mind

I thought I was ruined

In yours

I was cooling

Naked, Alone, & Unafraid

An original novel waiting to be written

Unseen to me but you knew

Infusing

Transfusing

Reintroducing imaginativeness

Inserting hues of pigments

Dancing rose

Pigeon toed turquoise

Stomping yellow who likes to be called gold

Bristol canvas of sandpaper

Cutting to the bone of the beauty

That far too long my eyes have forgotten to see

Inside The Room

I'd rather be locked up in my room
Without a care in the word
A pen
A pad
A pencil
Some glue
Creating the limitations of a unlimited existence
Acrylic, clay, lamps, a broom
Clapping my hands to the rhythms of the pen
Dancing my cares away in view of the world
For all to see with a care
Canvases bright as the summer's night
Depicting creativity only found locked inside of me
Form verse form
Challenging every definition of truth
Life love
Satisfaction, hope desired, hope achieved
All found in my room where I'm locked away
I have the key
It really doesn't matter if you look at me crazy
Crazier than a coo-coo bird without a tree
My feelings ain't hurt at all
You never loved or even liked me for me
Don't be acting concerned now that I

Naked, Alone, & Unafraid

Locked myself away with the only key

Peace in the silence

Happiness in the fumes

Of my acrylic hitting canvases between the brushes of affection

Just so that you know I care

You are not involved in this

I'm not inviting you into my happiness

Find your own

Satisfaction came with a song

Center of my peace it the center of my piece

I know I'm to be concerned about you

But you disappoint the reality I seek

Reality f meekness, humbleness, hermit-tality

Amish simplicity depicting a lifestyle

Embracing the things that encompass my very existence

Never letting down or disappointing me

Always allowing me to see the beauty in the simplicity

Surrounding me

In my room

With my pen and pad

Lost without my creativity

I am fine

Thank you

And close the door behind you

I Feel For You

I feel for you

But I don't know if I love you

I'm feeling you

But I'm not sure how this is

Supposed to go

I want to say that my loins aren't aching

That your kisses don't consume me

They do

They are

I'm unsure though

Of if I am responding as I should

Decisions

Decisively indecisive

Nowhere to go but gotta go

Looking around as the world seemingly passes me by

 Not moving from this couch until I decide

I will sit here and watch my days turn to night

Just to become day again

Realizing that my couch is darn comfortable

And life stops

At least for the moment

I think of you

Lord

Don't let this be a dream

Or just a momentary thing

To hope for love is hopeless unless love can be realized

Lord

I live for you

I breathe for you

 I dream of pleasing you

Yet I am here

Trying to determine the days

How exactly each hour is supposed to lay

Hearing melodies in my heart

"But, C... it's only been a few weeks."

Naked, Alone, & Unafraid

I know! I Know!

I keep telling myself

I won't even go there in this moment

A muse is a muse

I choose to let my muse amuse me

If I have to choose a path not traditionally done

Then that's the way I go

Easy talks

Difficulty lies in my wondering if I am being

Enough

Authentic, worldly, Godly, woman, feminine, thin,

Just enough to be pleasing to you

Will I scare you off with the truth of me?

It's not that my past is such a secret

Like the sopranos where I go and do whatever

My past is my past yet so presently future

My past laid the foundation of my life

My past taught me not to regret

Though there are things I wonder about

Like now would I be different if I...

I find myself back at a point of acceptance

Feeling like I have accepted me but now do you

Would my promiscuity scare thee?

Be number 1 or 103

Would my mind trick you into manipulation of my way?

Would the voluptuousness of my hips keep you

If they jiggled like gelatin cellulite?

My eyes are bigger than most

I feet are small for my height

I have a mind, an imagination, a dream, a desire

A voice that will be heard

One way or another

I would selfishly give me last in expectation of yours

The selflessly let you go first because I just want to

I could go on and on about my faults

But this not to tear me down and lift you p

I just want to know if you can really deal with me

Handle me

Love me unconditionally

Yes your mind intrigues me

As smart and little yellow bus it is at times

But you keep me laughing

You keep me smiling

You keep me guessing

There is no right or wrong way about this

It just is

I am ok with that

I am like totally cool with it

No prob!

Are You Ready For the Shift?

Malachi 3:7B

Moving towards God

People think Malachi is about giving tithes

But it is about giving God the best we have

That nothing can be substituted

The best must be given to God

Are you giving God your best?

Not your lame, crippled sacrifice

But truly the best sacrifice you can give him?

The sacrifice of praise

Of tithe

Of giving your time

Even at work I see how my best must get better

How I have to improve my gift

It's not just the money

It's the attitude about the money

The shift is on

Money is flowing from the heavenly

Not just money but position and stature

God is calling those out who are faithful

Time is still available for moving forward

Must turn to God now

Must move in God now

No distractions

No reason not to move forward in God

God is making available everything, so you can't worry

About the material stuff

There is no need to.

Naked, Alone, & Unafraid

New Meaning of Friendship

Holding hands

Laying side by side

Intimacy may not be marriage material

Yet the depth of our connection

Make strangers walk up and ask us when our wedding day is

Gazing into your brown eyes

Gives me a sense of peace

Feeling like I am wrapped in a security blanket within your arms

And yes

I did exhale

The opinions of others did not matter

Needing you by my side was more important to me

Until we went out

And you introduced me

"Yeah, this is my friend…."

Ummm… Excuse me?

"Have you met my friend?"

He says again to someone new

What kind of games are you playing here?

Did you not just sleep over last night?

In that moment

My world stopped spinning

I was standing with a silly grin on my face

Hand extended

Wishing they were instead around your neck

Going throughout the night

Confused by the declaration of

The lack of love

We have

Second guessing everything that occurred between us before this moment

Was I a fling?

Did I just become that girl?

Who you never really wanted to commit to

As you are searching for your next best thing

I think I did

I drop your hand and walk away slyly

Really fuming on the inside

Trying to hide the disgust from

A face that never hides anything

Only for you to follow me

Feeling your hand on the small of my back

Again

I just gaze at the wonderful art

At the High

Textures at angles that would confuse the common man

Imagine the added pressure behind my eyes as I tried to decipher

The deeper meaning

Of the painting

And us

Walking away again

Only to have you at my heels

I turn to look at you

Your eyes danced as mine threw flames

A smile crossed your face

Bestowing the sweetest of love upon my face

Tilting my head to the right

As I look upon your face

The face of the man whom I thought I would love

Forever

Blinking away my disappointment I say

"So we are friends?"

Moment of truth

Confusion or maybe fear took its place on the stage of his face

"Huh? I mean yeah. Of course we are friends."

As he begins to stare at another piece of art

"That is news to me."

Was my reply as he reached out

Hugging me around my waist

A very public display

Of the affection shown in a greater measure

In the dark

"You are one of my closest friends."

He whispers in my ear

Pushing me from behind

To the next display of art

"Interesting..."

I reply

Staring into oblivion

Tranquil colors surrounding the canvas

Hearing the music of the museum

Feeling the sense of culture and admiration

Not looking separated but feeling divided within my heart

As he began to push me towards the next painting

I grabbed his hands and turned myself around to face him

Looking up into those almond brown eyes

Not seeing even a lack of love for me in them

Naked, Alone, & Unafraid

Though he gazed

He could not understand the hurt in my eyes

"Let me show you how I am with my friends."

I take his hand

Dropping them by his side

And walk away.

Naked, Alone, and Unafraid

Today is a day that I have felt before
July 7th, 2005
September 11th, 2001
Three years, ten months, and four days
Since the bombing in New York
I remember that I was working in the career center
It was my junior year
That was the place of my work study
I went through the morning moving as usual
Not turning the TV on at all before I leave
I go to work and am greeted by solemn faces
They tell me about the first plane
I see the second plane
I watch as both buildings fall one at a time
I cry
I can't stop
It started when they first told me of the attack
And it wouldn't stop
I kept crying
Nothing in my heart and mind could
Prepare me for this event
That was so close to home yet so far away
It's not like I had any family in London
I didn't have any in New York

Yet the feeling is the same

Alone, hurt, scared, afraid

Wanting some type of understanding

Some type of condolence

I remember leaving the student center to go back to my apartment

My fellow students were chillin'

Laughing, having fun like any other day

Yet I felt cold and alone

How could they just stand there?

Did they not care?

Is there no sympathy in their beings?

"PEOPLE JUST DIED!!""

I want to yell

"CARE!!"

Then I ran into my classmate from DC

We hugged

I asked about his family

He said they were ok

We talked briefly but it helped me

And I knew he was glad that someone cared

We hugged again and went our separate ways

At home, I prayed

I prayed for the lives of those who were lost

For those who were still alive

For this great nation of mine

I prayed

I remember sitting on my couch as I am right now

Watching the news

Writing

Praying

As I watched into the early morning

CNN, MCNBC, ABC

All channels the same

My heart hurt then

Just like does today

I leave for London in 19 days

Not know the situation

What it will be at that time

Yet knowing that I will be closer

To the situation than ever before

It will be literally in front of me

It will be cleaned up

Looking nice again

But people died

People were hurt

And I will fee that

Why at this time in my life will this come to be Lord?

Why must I see, feel, and go through this experience?

I don't want you to take it away

But I am just wondering what I am going to be learning

What must I be open to?

Though it's different locations

Naked, Alone, & Unafraid

Different attacks

The feeling is still there

Here I am sitting alone on my couch

Where is the love?

Naked, Alone, & Unafraid

About The Author

Candace Eldridge has a passion for self-expression of lifestyle shown in her businesses, which focus on art and real estate. Candace is the Artist that Loves Real Estate. To fulfill this passion, Candace helps others identify their ideal lifestyle and helps them to create a plan to accomplish these goals. She has worked in Electrical Sales, Commercial Leasing, and Residential Sales for over 11 years. Her art has been sold to individuals from Japan to Las Vegas. She has also performed her Poetry and has various gallery showings around Atlanta.

Candace Eldridge currently resides in Atlanta, GA. She enjoys traveling, cooking, and being around her loved ones. She cherishes every opportunity to reflect and be grateful. Her poetry idols are Langston Hughes, Maya Angelou, Nikki Giovanni, Toni Morrison, Jill Scott, and Nina Simone.

You can follow via the following:

INSTAGRAM - @MS_CANDACE_BABY

FACEBOOK - @CLEARTISTRY

WEBSITE - HTTPS://CLEARTISTRY.WIXSITE.COM/HOME

EMAIL – CLEARTISTRY@GMAIL.COM

All artwork shown within this book is available in print and/or original canvas painting. Contact Candace Eldridge at CLEARTISTRY@GMAIL.COM regarding any painting you are interested in purchasing by citing the page number. Candace is also available for all custom commission projects as well.

Acknowledgements

This book would not have been possible without the help and guidance of the following people. I will never be able to thank you enough for your impact on our lives, our work, and this book.

Friends and Family

Thank you to my mom and dad, Kathy and Victor for loving me unconditionally. You guys provided me the space to grow into the woman I am today and the constant support for all of my life decisions. I am who I am because you are who you are. I love you!

Thank you to my sister Natasha for always have a vision and dream for the future. It was a result of reading your journals, the books you were in the middle of reading and even you providing me with my own journal that I kick started my writing experience as a teenager. I never met anyone who dreamed as boldly as you did nor actually went after those dreams and accomplished them. I am proud to be your little sister.

To my cousins Jonathan and Tamika; you both have been my rock while living in Atlanta. Growing into adults with you guys have shaped my life. You provide support when others didn't. You defended me. You supported all my endeavors. And your love has been and continues to be a bright shining light in my world. I couldn't and wouldn't have published this book with your support and belief in me.

To my friends in Atlanta, new and old, thank you. Quala, Kim, Ariana, TaWanda, Tamika, Jonathan, Robyn, Monica, Garden of Prayer, JR, J9 to name a few. Your support has meant the world to me. In the moments when I doubted myself, you stood in a place of support. You did not waiver, you did argue, you did not stop supporting or loving me. Thank you.

To my extended family of aunts, uncles, cousins, and friends. I thank you for your support! I love you all and have hugs galore for you when I see you!

Contributors

My manuscript reader, editor, and personal photographer is Ariana Richardson of Ariana Richardson Photography. Thank you for all of your valuable time and incredible feedback. You are forever a part of this book. You can learn more about Ariana at https://photosbyariana.com.

Kim Martin for helping with the editing of this book for print. Thank you for helping me to share it with the world. You can learn more about Kim at www.redefindingyou.com.

Gregg Brown with Skybox Cinema for taking some awesome photos of my art. I wouldn't have been able to present it to the world without you. You can learn more about Gregg at https://skyboxcinema.tv.

Naked, Alone, & Unafraid

Made in the USA
Columbia, SC
18 December 2018